The Driving Force

D1564224

THE DRIVING FORCE

Michel Tremblay

translated by

Linda Gaboriau

Talonbooks
Vancouver

Talonbooks
P.O. Box 2076, Vancouver, British Columbia, Canada V6B 3S3
www.talonbooks.com

Typeset in New Baskerville and printed and bound in Canada.

First Printing: 2005

LIBRARY AND ARCHIVES CANADA CATALOGUING IN PUBLICATION

Tremblay, Michel, 1942–
[Impératif présent. English]
    The driving force / Michel Tremblay ; translated by Linda Gaboriau.

Translation of: L'impératif présent.
A play.
ISBN 0-88922-530-3

    I. Gaboriau, Linda   II. Title.   III. Title: Impératif présent.   English.

PS8539.R47I4513 2005   C842'.54   C2005-902473-9

The publisher gratefully acknowledges the financial support of the Canada Council for the Arts; the Government of Canada through the Book Publishing Industry Development Program; and the Province of British Columbia through the British Columbia Arts Council for our publishing activities.

for Wajdi Mouawad

who suggested that I revisit the characters of
Alex and Claude in Le vrai monde?

L'impératif présent was first presented on October 17, 2003 at the Théâtre de Quat'Sous in Montreal with the following cast and crew:

ALEX: Jacques Godin
CLAUDE: Robert Lalonde

Director: André Brassard
Set design: Richard Lacroix
Costume design: Mérédith Caron
Lighting: Michel Beaulieu
Assistant Director: Isabelle Brodeur

CHARACTERS

ALEX, 77
CLAUDE, 55

ACT ONE

ALEX's room in a home for Alzheimer's patients.

ALEX is sitting in a wheelchair.

CLAUDE, his son, has just finished washing and dressing him and is patting his cheeks with eau de cologne.

ALEX will remain perfectly still, absent, during the entire act.

CLAUDE

You don't know what this takes out of me, do you? The physical effort … and all the rest … Washing you. Powdering you. Putting on your diaper, your clean pyjamas. Shaving you. Patting your cheeks with cologne. Just to cover up how you're going to smell in half an hour. So it won't stink the minute we open the door. To create the illusion that you're clean for a while.

He has finished grooming his father. He backs away from the chair and examines his work.

How long's it going to take before you start deteriorating again? Your brain has practically stopped working, but your heart goes on pumping like nothing was wrong. You always had a thick head of hair, and a heavy beard. If I weren't here to shave you ... They don't have the time around here, do they? I mean, they can't doll you up like I do, they can't devote the whole afternoon to you, they make it short and sweet, deal with the most pressing stuff, the most urgent, they've got other cases, worse cases, the bedridden ones who can't be moved ... They don't have time to climb into the tub with you to give you more than a sponge bath ... They'll oil your body every night so you don't get bedsores, but they won't climb into the tub with you to give you a bath ...

He leans over his father.

When that happens to you, when they can't move you anymore, when that time comes and you can't get out of your bed, I promise I'll go on shaving you. And patting your cheeks with cologne. (*Silence.*) It's called dignity. (*Silence.*) What are you thinking about? You must be thinking about something? I don't see how someone can stop thinking. Completely. Are you really not aware of anything? Not so long ago, you used to look at me with, I don't know, let's say a trace of intensity. You followed me around the room with your eyes. You didn't know who I was, but I was there, you saw me, and your eyes followed me. Now when I walk by you, you don't even blink. You look like an old, grouchy baby. Are you blind? Has your brain stopped sending messages to your eyes? Has it stopped telling your eyes that they should close once in a while, to lubricate them? When we put those drops in your eyes, can you feel them overflow and run down your cheeks? No, you can't, right? We have to wipe them to prevent them from running into your mouth because they could be poisonous. There's lead in eyedrops, and lead is dangerous. Think about it, when I was starting out, when I was a linotypist, I was the one who was facing lead poisoning. And now I'm putting lead in your eyes. I don't know how many gallons it would take for your body to finally react … for your heart to stop, or explode … But that would mean you'd have to have one. And it's too late for that, right? Today's not the day you're going to start having a heart … Actually, we can't even say it's too late. No. There was never a time for that. And even if you'd had a heart as big as the world, what would that change now? Right now, today, between the two of us? You'd still be in the same place. And so would I. I'd still come and do exactly the same things. We'd still be staring at each other, you in your diaper you've probably already started to dirty, and me, barely dry after our bath together. The only thing that would be different is our past. Our memories. But since you wouldn't have any memories, because you'd be in the same state, it wouldn't change a thing for you. Nothing would be different for you today, if you had been a devoted, loving father, so why weren't you? It wouldn't change a thing!

He moves away, goes to sit on the edge of his father's bed.

This afternoon, on my way here, I had some errands to do, I had to buy myself a pair of shoes, and at one point, I walked by Ogilvy's. It's weird how things happen, sometimes … Without thinking twice, really, I swear I didn't think about it, otherwise I would've felt stupid and I wouldn't have done it, but really, without thinking, I walked into Ogilvy's and headed straight for the perfume counter. Never saw so much perfume! The place smelled of wealthy women, like intermission at Place des Arts. Everything was shiny and chic, with glass and mirrors everywhere … They say our sense of smell triggers our memories best, so … I wanted to try even though I figured it was impossible … Anyway, I pounced on the first saleslady I saw, a pretty lady of a certain age, well-dressed, well-groomed, all neat and clean, with a big smile on her face because she probably figured she'd be sure to sell some expensive perfume to the middle-aged man who was heading toward her … for his pretty secretary, or his mistress, or maybe for his actual wife if he was as straightlaced as he looked … She didn't recognize me. Guess she never goes to the theatre. I went right up to her and without thinking, I swear, I asked her, "Does Lotus by Yardley still exist?" Honestly … I didn't even know if the Yardley company still existed! And you know what she said? "Even if it still existed, I doubt that we'd sell it here, sir. I think they used to sell it in drugstores." Is that true? I know, I can remember clearly that we bought yours at the drugstore, but is it true they didn't sell it anywhere else? One thing's for sure, it was pretty cheap. Every year, Ma would give me seventy-five cents and say, "It's your father's birthday next week, go buy him his bottle of Lotus by Yardley." Seventy-five cents plus tax. That's what your birthday present cost us. And it wasn't even me who paid for it. I'd ask them to gift-wrap it ... always the same drugstore paper with the little blue and gold flowers on a white background ... When I gave it to you, you'd always say the same thing, "Thanks, my boy! Exactly what I needed, hardly have any left! I was trying to make it last as long as I could. When an elastic band snaps in your face, you know you gotta throw it out, but you think you can make perfume last forever ... but sooner or later, the bottle's empty and you're stuck smelling your own smell! And in my profession, kid, you're better off not smelling natural, better to smell like flowers, a bouquet of roses, like a whole rose garden! A travelling salesman is more than a bee flying from flower to flower, he's a bee that brings flowers to flowers." And you'd douse yourself with the stuff. You put it on your handkerchiefs, your shirt collars and cuffs … Behind your back, Ma always said you used so much of it, when you came out of the bathroom, sometimes the air was so thick you could cut it with a knife. And she was almost right! I'm telling you, we could smell you coming from way off. In your car, in the winter, we'd suffocate, it smelled so strong. Sometimes I'd walk by your bedroom and say to myself, "I guess he's back," because I could smell you. But most of the time, it was just a faint whiff, a trace Ma hadn't managed to get rid of, a smell that wouldn't go away … A couple of times I heard her say, on the phone, "Alex smells like a funeral parlour! And it's our own fault." And … this afternoon … that's what I was looking for. That smell. I can't remember it. At all. I couldn't tell you what it smelled like, I just remember it smelled strong. What does a real lotus flower smell like? Maybe I could've gone to a florist's, but I don't know if they sell them. This time of the year, or any time. And I wanted to see if what they say about our sense of smell is true, not with real flowers but with my memory of Lotus by Yardley. Not the real smell, I forgot that ages ago, but … Maybe opening the bottle, just now, after shaving you, things would've come back to me all of a sudden …

He comes back to his father's wheelchair and crouches down beside him.

Because I want you to know that I stopped hating you recently. And I was hoping that Lotus by Yardley would jump-start my motor again. Because I feel numb when I'm with you now. I don't feel a thing when I look at you, and I miss those first times when we were in the tub together and I wanted to drown you. I'm getting close to forgiving you, and that makes my head spin. Because I don't want to. Because that's the last thing I want. Not as long as you're still alive!

He moves away from his father.

When Mariette came to set you up here, I hadn't seen either one of you for ages. I hadn't even been in touch with you for a long time. I'd decided to forget I ever had a father, and as for my sister, she's such an incurable nighthawk, I never know when to call her … Listen to me … as if that were any reason to lose touch with your sister … It sounds like one of our old family myths … the incident is true, but there's so much icing on it, no way you can find the truth. I didn't see the two of you anymore because I didn't feel like seeing you, period! The last time I saw you was at Ma's funeral. And I said to myself, "Never again! Never!" You dared go to her funeral, acting like a grief-stricken widower, after spending your life practically laughing in her face, after cheating on her, humiliating her, treating her like your servant who kept your slippers warm while the master went out to play! They made us sit together on the same bench in the church, even though I didn't want to—I was sitting on your left, and Mariette on your right. When you started crying, heaving your shoulders, I thought you were laughing, that you'd finally let the cat out of the bag, that you were unable to hide your relief at being free, at last, after all those years in the prison your family had represented to you … But no, you were crying, you were sobbing like a loving husband.

You kept it up for the whole ceremony. You were still mocking her in her coffin. Shameless, sure you'd never be punished, sure you'd come out on top as usual! Even the relatives who never liked you were touched. Poor Alex has lost his Madeleine, he loved her so much. I felt like standing up and exposing you right there in the middle of the church. But it wasn't the right time or place, it was the funeral of the most important person in my life, so I decided to spare you. But I also decided I'd never lay eyes on you again. And I kept my word. Anyway, I admit it was a shock when I saw you again after all those years. Mariette had warned me, but ... nothing can prepare you for this kind of thing. You tell yourself: it won't be that bad, I'll get through it. I wanted to visit you while you were still conscious. Just in case. In case, something might happen. But what happened wasn't what I expected ... You were already suffering from aphasia. Not only had I never seen someone suffering from aphasia, but it was happening to my father who'd spent his life holding forth, delivering his endless speeches, drowning us, and the truth, in a flow of words, a dense logorrhoea fuelled by alcohol and the desire to trick people, to get his own way. You could hardly manage to say a few words, you had to concentrate, we could see in your eyes how hard it was, and then, instead of the word, "hello," for instance, you'd come out with the word "helper" or the word "jello" … When I came into this room, you were expecting me, Mariette told you I was coming. You stood up beside your bed, you looked me straight in the eye, you concentrated, I could feel the muscles around your mouth straining, and you said, "Jello!" It was pathetic, it was devastating, I felt like I'd been hit with a ton of bricks, for sure, but at the same time … At the same time, I couldn't help but think it was a strange twist of fate, almost poetic justice, that the great sweet-talker, the big gabber, the king of eloquence couldn't even find the words to say hello! I spent, I don't know how long, maybe two hours, with you that day. And you didn't manage to say ten sentences. I could read the humiliation on your face because you still had periods when you were completely conscious, totally aware, and you were mortified to have me see you in that state

… I told you to talk with your hands, that I realized you were having trouble pronouncing words, and that only made you feel more embarrassed. Then, at a certain point, during a silence that lasted too long, I could see in your eyes that you thought I was happy to see you like that, and that I was staying here so I could enjoy your humiliation, as if the thought that crossed my mind when I arrived had stayed with me, and I wasn't leaving because I was happy you were aphasic. And you know what? I found that so outrageous, I didn't even bother to contradict you, or to defend myself. I thought, "If he's dumb enough to think that, let him think it." But maybe I was kidding myself? What do you think? Were you the one who was right, in the end? Did you see something in me that I'd censored the minute I thought it, because I found it too ugly? Were those first two hours the nightmare I remember today, or have I just buried the pleasure I felt under the layer of pain, the layer of sadness a good son is supposed to feel under the circumstances? We'll never know, will we? Because it's too late for you—and I'd never dare face something like that. Even if I find myself doing things I never would've imagined I could do since I started coming here regularly. Some nice things people might say are due to a natural generosity, and other things … like what's going on right now, and every time I come to visit … talking like this, rattling on to a dying man who's lost his mind, paying him back, day after day, for his pointless speeches, with more pointless speeches, talk, talk, talking, till I drop, to an inert body, with no hope of remission, on your side or mine, because one of the two parties has withdrawn permanently. I'm exhausted when I leave here, my throat is raw, my nerves are shot, because I dare say out loud things I'd never dare write in my plays because I'd find them either too melodramatic, or too dull! I write crazy, badly constructed, wildly lyrical plays for you, three afternoons a week, and you can't even appreciate them or dismiss them with a wave of your hand and a sarcastic grin, the way you did with everything I've ever written. I make you listen to talk you would've hated, but in the final analysis, I'm punishing myself because I know you're in no state to accept it or reject it. But, at the same time, it's become my new motor! My punishment has become my driving force! Instead of talking to you in my head, the way I did for most of my life, I can do it for real now, even if I know that I'll never be able to convince you of anything! I'll never convince you that I'm talented or that what I write is any good! All my life I've tried to avoid writing to please the critics or the experts, I've just focussed on the play I had to write, concentrated on what I thought I had to say, and refused to think about what so-and-so might say about this sentence or that speech ... but all along I knew I was kidding myself, that there was always one person I wanted to please, one person I needed to convince, like when I wrote my very first play ... You committed the most violent act I've ever seen anyone commit—you destroyed the only manuscript of an author's first play. You burned my first play, page by page, with your lighter, with no scruples, no regrets, with the clear conscience of a man who's convinced he's right! You destroyed my play because you were convinced you were right, just like I was convinced

I was right to denounce you in my play. I could have rewritten it, I knew it by heart, it was a short play, probably not very good, but I chose to drop it, and to keep that blow intact, like a burn that never heals, and over the years I realized that it had become my motor. I'd never be able to forgive you for committing that act, and as long as forgiveness was impossible, I'd have a reason to write. I wanted every play I wrote, every bit of my work, every successful production to be a blow to you, as painful, as brutal as the one you dealt me before my career had even begun. You wanted to crush me in the bud, you failed, and now I was going to try to crush you, slowly but surely, bit by bit, success after success after success! I had my first taste of revenge ten years ago, do you remember? No, even if your brain was still working you wouldn't remember, because you were so caught up in your little triumph, so intoxicated by your fifteen minutes of fame that you didn't notice a thing. There was a TV show back then where five nights in a row, they'd invite a celebrity to come meet people from his past—relatives, teachers, classmates ... When my turn came, when they invited me, I saw an opportunity to stage a double-revenge, and I succeeded.

I asked them to invite all my classmates from the ninth grade, the class that had been the meanest, the most violent with me, and I forced thirty guys who'd always made fun of me, who'd pushed me around and insulted me, to come say nice things about me on television, how much they'd liked me, what a funny, intelligent, sociable guy I was at fifteen ... It was the price they had to pay to be on television and almost all of them accepted! One after the other, they showed up with a story probably invented by the producers of the show, one of them even came out with a flattering nickname that nobody had ever called me! They all arrived with a big smile on their face, to praise their great friend Claude who they missed so much. "We should get together, it's crazy, it's been so long ... " You can imagine what a great week I spent! And the last night, the Friday night, was the supreme moment, thanks to your presence, much appreciated by everyone. And you, too, just to be on television and enjoy your fifteen minutes of fame, were willing to come and tell everyone how great I was. I don't know how they managed to track you down in some tavern, but they did and you accepted, right away. I wasn't surprised that Mariette came to perpetuate the image of the ideal family that's remained her theme song till this day, so she can avoid seeing things like they are, to spare herself the pain. That was to be expected—sad, but to be expected. But you! You came to say nice things about me! About my writing! In public! You dragged out your old Fuller Brush Man act, your travelling salesman tricks, your gift for telling dirty jokes, and within seconds you were hogging the stage, you were funny, you were smart, you wallowed in your pride, let everyone know how proud you were to have given birth to such a talented son, you even suggested my great talent probably came from your side of the family, and even, especially, from you! To hear you talk, you had nurtured my talent, cultivated it like a delicate flower, you'd almost guided my hand when I started writing plays, when what you really did was destroy the first one with your own two hands. There was no stopping you, you believed every poetic word you said, and you kept winking at me like we were in cahoots! You kept winking at me, like we were buddies, on television! What a victory! It was one of the greatest moments in my life! (*Silence.*) Not all the time, but often enough, when I was writing there'd come a moment when I'd think, "This play will kill him! If it works, it'll rub more salt in the wound." I wasn't writing to impress the critics, I was writing to get back at you!

He takes a straight-backed chair and sets it down beside his father's wheelchair.

I'll never admit that anywhere but here! I'll go on explaining my work with all sorts of sidetracks, circumlocutions, digressions and paraphrasing, but no one else will know what really drives me, what I could lose if I forgive you. If I cave in. If I soften up because of what's happened to you. (*Silence.*) I arrived here one afternoon ... It smelled pretty bad. It was actually awful ... I went to speak to someone at the nurse's desk, I asked them how they could leave my father like that when he needed someone to clean him up ... The nurse had bags under her eyes, she'd been working for eighteen hours straight, she could hardly stand up, she explained that there had been emergencies, real emergencies, that your turn was coming, but not right away … I asked her if the bathroom was free, if I had the right to bathe you myself. She said: "Of course, but are you sure you can do it? It's harder than you think, you know, your father's no featherweight." I came back here with a wheelchair, a little bar of soap and a towel … Just transferring you from your bed to the wheelchair was quite a job, and I started wondering what I'd gotten myself into … In the hallway, I looked like a devoted son, the nurse nodded at us and looked grateful as we went by. There was a doctor, too, who talked to me about my last play, and ended up saying that everyone on the floor knew you were my father … I felt like saying that sure didn't get you any preferential treatment, that was clear from the way you smelled, but I bit my tongue … Once we were in the bathroom, I realized that the person who'd taken a bath before you, or the person who'd given him the bath, hadn't bothered to clean the tub, so I found myself down on my knees, on the tile floor, scrubbing the rusty porcelain, trying to get rid of the filth left by a perfect stranger ... By the time I'd finished and the tub was more or less acceptable, I was already exhausted ... My back ached, I was sweating ... I screwed up my nerve and I undressed you the best I could ... Undressing someone in a wheelchair isn't easy, even if they're only wearing pyjamas and a diaper ... It was the first time I'd ever seen a diaper for adults ... It was the first time I'd ever changed a dirty diaper, since I never had any kids ... I was trying not to look at what I saw, trying to think about something else, telling myself that neither one of us ever would've thought we'd see the day ... Once you were undressed ... I don't know ... suddenly I didn't know what to do with you ... How to wash you ... should I stick you in the tub and do it, acre by acre, as Ma used to say, or put you under the shower? ... I really didn't know what to do ... Good intentions are great, but ... Before I knew what I was doing, I took off all my clothes, I turned on the shower, took you into my arms and got under the shower ... (*Long silence.*)

Once we were both good and wet, I didn't know how to go about washing you, but I finally managed to kneel in the tub and set you down, so my hands were free ... (*Another moment of silence.*) I started to lather you, beginning with your head, your face, your neck ... You smelled a bit better and that encouraged me ... After I lathered your chest, I noticed your legs ... What a shock! I have the same legs, exactly the same legs as you. The same knees. The same feet. Your penis even looks like mine. From the waist down, the two of us are identical! I inherited Ma's face, but I got your lower body. It was crazy! I felt like I was washing myself, but without feeling the soap on my thighs, on my calves, on my feet ... I'd closed your eyes because I was afraid you wouldn't do it yourself and the soap would sting without your realizing it ... I washed you from head to toe ... Now I know every part of your body like a mother with her baby. (*Silence.*) Then, there in the tub, with the warm water running, rinsing, washing everything away, I thought, "This is it, this is the real moment of catharsis! It can happen right here, today. If I want, this could be the moment of forgiveness." We

31

were in the position of *La Pietà*! You were my child and I was your mother! A Pietà beneath a shower of warm water! And if I wanted, I could forgive you. And it would be done, once and for all. (*Silence.*) But I didn't feel a thing. Absolutely nothing. I felt no—I don't know if the word generosity is the right word, but I didn't feel inclined to be generous. I looked at your sex, and I thought, "That's where I came from, but the minute I left his body, I was of no importance to him, so why should I forgive him? Why should I be generous to a man who was never generous to anyone, who always thought only of himself, never realizing there were other people around?" I felt absolutely nothing toward you, even though I was holding you in my arms. (*Silence.*) Then suddenly, out of nowhere, without even looking for it, my hatred for you came back, it hit me like a ton of bricks, and I started to shake. A second earlier, I'd felt nothing, and the next thing I knew, I was trembling with hatred. It would have been easy to kill you right then and there! To drop you in the tub on purpose, so you'd pass out or drown in a couple of inches of water ... Then run to get help, sobbing, shouting there'd been an accident, looking like a hero, the devoted son who'd wanted to cleanse his father of his own excrement, but he was inexperienced and he drowned him, the poor boy! (*Silence.*) But I realized ... not only did I not want to forgive you, on top of that, I needed you, your physical presence, to keep my motor running. Your being gone would be like your being forgiven. Useless. It's your presence in my life that's useful. It's always been that way. Wherever I was, I could always tell myself that, even if I didn't know exactly where you were, you weren't far away, that you were there in the background, spying on me, sneering at me, and that you still weren't convinced, that you'd never be convinced, and I'd always have someone to convince, you, and that's what kept me going! (*Silence.*) So I'm keeping you alive. I'm the one who's keeping you alive.

He stands up, walks away from his father.

But recently ... I don't know ... I can feel myself wavering ... The more I see you in this state—or maybe simply because you're no longer aware of

33

anything, so you're no longer useful for anything—
I feel like I'm on the verge of committing the
irreparable. Forgiving you. Why? Because I'm fed
up with coming here, or because I'm more human
than I thought, or because I want to move on to
something else. But what? You've been behind
everything I've done in my life! Behind every play,
every success, every flop, there was an attempt to
convince you, to rub your nose in my success, and
to say, "You see, a person can do something with
his life despite the presence of someone like you!"
But it wasn't despite! It was because! Because of
the presence of someone like you!

*He walks back to his father and leans over
his chair.*

Don't leave! Stay! Hang on! Even unconscious,
stay! I need you! I'm afraid I won't be able to do
anything if you're gone, or if I forgive you! Don't
die! It will leave a hole at the heart of my being!

*He straightens up and goes back to sit on the
edge of his father's bed.*

Sometimes when I walk out of here, I'm convinced
that you get out of your chair the minute I close

the door, and that you start dancing, and laughing and clapping your hands. That you laugh at me behind my back, like you have all your life! And I come running back, I fling open the door ... and I'm disappointed every time.

He prepares to leave.

Enough of this emotional stuff, that'll do for today. Got to save some for next time ... I didn't tell you about the weather ... It's a strange day. The sky is completely white. Like there's a white bell over the city, and it hurts your eyes. The sun's not out, but you have to wear sunglasses ... At least I do, it gives me migraines if I don't. (*Silence.*) I'll be back to give you your bath on Friday.

He exits.

ALEX remains alone for some fifteen seconds.

CLAUDE flings open the door, looks at his father.

Blackout.

ACT TWO

CLAUDE's room in a home for Alzheimer's patients.

CLAUDE is sitting in a wheelchair.

ALEX, his father, has just finished washing and dressing him and is patting his cheeks with eau de cologne.

CLAUDE will remain perfectly still, absent, during the entire act.

ALEX

You don't know what this takes out of me, do you? The physical effort ... and all the rest ... Washing you. Powdering you. Putting on your diaper, your clean pyjamas. Shaving you. Patting your cheeks with cologne. Just to cover up how you're going to smell in half an hour. So it won't stink the minute we open the door. To create the illusion that you're clean for a while.

He has finished grooming his son. He backs away from the chair and examines his work.

How long's it going to take before you start deteriorating again? Your brain has practically stopped working, but your heart goes on pumping like nothing was wrong. You always had a thick head of hair, and a heavy beard. Do you remember how I hit the roof, in 1964, when you decided to grow your phoney artist's beard? I didn't want any bearded creeps in my house! I told you you'd look like a peace-and-love guitar-picker, and I was right, you did! Like a guitar-picker and a bum! I didn't want my kid to be a bum. But he was. Except he didn't play the guitar, he wrote plays! And not just any old plays! Anyway, if I wasn't here to shave you, today ... Can't the big shots who run this place find time to take care of you? You should've seen how uptight they looked just now, when I went to tell them you stank to high heaven ... Apparently they're tired, poor babies, there were some emergencies ... Are they going to wait till you've got bedsores before they take care of you around here? I'm gonna file a report, you just wait ... Do they think I've got nothing better to do than to give you a bath and change your diapers? I'm seventy-seven and in good health, I got better things to do in life than come here to take care of my son who's dragging out his death. I'm a retired man, not a nurse!

He leans over his son.

When they can't move you anymore, when that time comes and you can't get out of your bed, then I'll let your goddamn beard grow. You can leave this world looking like you looked at the beginning of your great career! That'll be my goodbye present. But until then, I'm gonna shave you! (*Silence.*) What are you thinking about? I don't get how someone can stop thinking. Completely. Are you really not aware of anything? Not so long ago, you still seemed to recognize me. You followed me around with your eyes. You knew who I was when I arrived and you watched me with this strange look in your eyes because you must've wondered what I was doing here. Now when I walk by, you don't even blink. Are you blind? Does this disease make you blind, too? It must be really boring, eh? … So if you're not aware of anything … I guess that makes you a vegetable who used to write mishmash. (*A loud and long laugh.*) If you could hear me, you'd tell me, as usual, that I've got no heart! You spent your life saying I had no heart! Well, I'm here, aren't I, isn't that proof that I've got one? If the roles were reversed and I was in your place, would you show up three times a week to give me my bath, change my diaper, shave me, pat my cheeks with cologne? Would you? No! You'd probably be off somewhere stabbing me in the back in one of your goddamn plays … I know you! I know who I was dealing with all those years, you lousy leech! You'd steal the last crumbs of my life! So you could make money with them!

He moves away, goes to sit on the edge of his son's bed.

I was walking down Saint Catherine Street this afternoon, before taking the metro to come here … I sold my car ages ago, I'd rather drink what little money I have … Even if I have to take it easy now, I'm no spring chicken, can't drink like I used to … Anyway, at one point, I was walking by Ogilvy's. I started thinking about your Aunt Tititte, everyone in the family thought she was so chic because she sold gloves at Ogilvy's … She was another hothead, that one … Anyway, I walked into the store without thinking … It was like I had an idea, but didn't know what yet … It's strange how our heads work sometimes … First thing I knew, I was walking up to the perfume counter … The place smelled so strong, I felt weak in the knees, for Chrissakes. Then suddenly I realized what I'd come for. I stood there facing this saleslady, who by the way reminded me a lot of your Aunt Tititte, like, after all these years, they still use the same mould for the salesladies at Ogilvy's … Anyway, I stood there and asked her if she had Lotus perfume by Yardley. You remember that stuff? That's what you used to give me for my birthday, Lotus by Yardley. She looked at me with her big eyes, like I came from the backwoods of Nominingue county, and she said: "I don't know if it still exists, sir, but even if it did, I doubt that we'd sell it here. I think they used to sell it in drugstores." Did you buy my birthday present at the drugstore? You never told me that! No wonder it stank! I bet it didn't even cost a buck. Is that all I was worth to the three of you? A buck? For you, your sister and your mother, it came out to thirty-three cents each. When I saw you coming, your hair slicked back, wearing your little suit, with your goddamn present in your hands, I felt like slapping you in the face! Lotus by Yardley! It smelled like a ton of rotten flowers, for Chrissakes! And it turned on my skin after a couple of hours! It made me smell sour! But after a while, I found a smart way to use your goddamn perfume. It became my alibi. How 'bout that! It hid the other smells, the smell of the other women I'd meet on my route as a "Fuller Brush Man," as you so kindly used to say. As soon as I got outside Montreal, at the beginning of my route, in Papineauville most of the time, because I always spent the first night there, I'd take a long shower to get rid of the unbelievable stink, and I'd do the opposite on my way home—I'd douse myself with your damn Lotus by Yardley on my way back into Montreal, and it would hide the nice smell of the other women! You used to say you could smell me coming from way off, and it was true! But not for the reason you thought! Your father wasn't as thick as you thought! I used the family present to cover my tracks. And you

know what? If I'd found some Lotus this
afternoon, you know what I would've done? Can
you see me coming? I bet you can, 'cause you're
smart too. That's right, I would've bought a bottle
and you would have spent your dying days
smelling like your father! The supreme insult.
(*Silence.*) No, maybe I wouldn't have gone that far,
even if I did go and ask if it still existed ...
(*Silence.*) But not out of kindness, no, maybe just
not to be reminded of the past. If you really want
to know, I don't want to remember that smell,
ever. (*Silence.*) Today's the only thing that matters,
kid. Not yesterday! How many times have I told
you that? But you ... even as a kid, you loved to
ruminate on what happened the day before, and
the day before that, and back in the days of
Methuselah! And you ended up earning your
living doing it! Did you ever live your own life, eh?
Did you? Did you have your own crises,
disappointments, joys? Or were you too busy
sniffing at other people's dirty underwear to have
a life of your own? Well, now it's your underwear
that smells bad! And believe me, nobody would
want to see a play about that!

He comes back to his son's wheelchair and crouches down beside him.

I want you to know something ... I've got a problem these days ... It feels like I've stopped being mad at you. That's why I lay it on, why I exaggerate when I come to see you ... I need to rev up my motor, you understand. Because I feel numb with you. I don't feel a thing when I look at you, and I miss those first times when I was shaving you and I felt like slitting your throat with the razor. Because I couldn't understand why I was doing all this for you. (*Silence.*) I'm getting close to forgiving you, that's the problem, and it makes my head spin. Because that's the last thing I want. I refuse to forgive you, because I want you to die before that happens! Afterwards, I'll figure out a way to forget. Not forgive. Forget.

He moves away from his son.

When Mariette found you here, 'cause she'd heard you were sick, it had been ages since I'd seen either one of you. We hadn't been in touch for a long time. Not since your mother's funeral, actually. Since the last time you missed the whole

46

point. When you misunderstood, as usual, what was happening. I felt you tense up sitting there beside me when I started to cry, because you couldn't, you couldn't, but mostly, you didn't want to see my grief. Real grief. My world was turned inside out. The loss! You never wanted to see how much I loved your mother, how much I adored her, despite my shortcomings, my faults, and I could feel you fuming there beside me because I dared cry at her funeral. I felt like standing up, taking you by the scruff of the neck, and throwing you onto your mother's coffin, insisting that you beg her forgiveness! That you beg her to forgive you for misunderstanding her, because you misunderstood me! For underestimating her intelligence! For not understanding what went on between the two of us and that it was none of your business! For spending your life interpreting other people instead of trying to understand yourself! Did you ever think that maybe I wasn't the one who made your mother sick? Eh? But I decided not to do it. It wasn't the right time. Or the right place. Maybe I should have. You and your success. That day I decided I'd cut you and your career out of my life, once and for all. And Mariette finally burned her bridges too ... Maybe after reading what a bastard I was in your plays ... There's so much icing in them, so many half-assed assumptions, so many false interpretations, it's impossible to find the truth in all that. (*Long silence.*) You don't know what it's like ... You don't know how it feels to be scared every time they announce your son's written a new play ... Every time, I think, "What's he gonna come out with this time ... Will I be the cause of all his misery again? Didn't he settle that in the last play, or that other one, two years ago?" And sure enough, there was always at least one little jab, a scene or a line about the horrible father who was the source of all unhappiness ... I admit that maybe that's all I could see. I was looking for it, and I found it ... and I was satisfied. Well, maybe not satisfied, but you know what I mean ... (*Silence.*) That's right, I went to see your plays, for sure ... I couldn't stop myself. I wanted to know what I was up against. And if you ask me, the good ones were never as good as the critics said. And the bad ones were never bad enough for me! (*Silence.*) There was one time, though, when I thought I could take my revenge ... I had the golden opportunity, but I didn't take advantage of it. Like at your mother's funeral. They'd invited me on television, to pay homage to you. I don't know how they managed to find me in the east end of Montreal where I ended up after I retired because it was cheaper ... Anyway, it was a show where they brought celebrities together with people who knew them before they were famous ... At first I refused, then, I thought, "Why not go denounce him on TV, get it off my chest, once and for all ... Why not tell everyone what a bastard he is, a lousy hypocrite and a liar." I could see myself, on TV, embarrassing you in front of everyone, telling them how you made a living off of us, off of our lives, and that I wasn't sure you had one of your own ... I could imagine you blushing, then turning white, then crying and starting to throw up right there in the studio 'cause you were so ashamed ... I thought, "The perfect revenge. What a great way to put an end to it all." Then, you know what? I decided to be generous, one last time, and to do exactly what you expected me to do: play the clown. I went and played the clown! And you know what? It was a lot of fun! The more I laid it on, the more I could see you squirming in your seat, and the more fun I had. I could see you were afraid of what I might say, and I loved it. But I did you the favour of not saying anything. One of the many favours I've done for you that you never noticed. I was playing the role they wanted me to play, the father, not too educated, who's happy to be on television, so he can crack his jokes in front of everyone. And I did it. Willingly and with pleasure! I got a real kick out of it! If you were still conscious, you'd figure out a way to believe that I lost my nerve at the last minute, but it's not true. Just the opposite! What I did was brave! Especially saying nice things about you! About your *theatre*! I talked about how relevant your plays are, how good your dialogue is, how poetic. Ha! If only they could've read my mind and seen what I was really thinking! How much I hate all that, how I think it really stinks! You stank before you started shitting your pants, you know that? (*Silence.*) When the show was over, a couple of technicians came to see me and told me how good I was, how I was the most natural of everyone who'd been on that week. I told them, "You're right, I was good, but don't go thinking I was natural!" You just muttered a vague thanks and took off with your friends ... You couldn't even look me in the eye! You knew you'd had a close call, but you didn't know how close! For ten minutes, I'd had you at my mercy, I could've destroyed you with a couple of cutting remarks, like the ones you've been making about me for years in your plays, but I did you a favour, a real favour, Claude, I let you go on thinking what you think of me. It was a very generous gesture. And I've never regretted it. You earned your living with your so-called truth, but I was the only one who knew the real truth, and I decided to keep it to myself. So you could go on earning your living! I could've landed you in the street, Claude! (*Silence.*) Anyway, I gotta admit it was a shock when I found you here after all those years ... I'm still your father, right? ... And I was determined to visit you while you were still conscious. Mariette had to explain what "aphasic" meant, and I thought to myself, "For once, when he sees me walk in, he won't be able to start yelling his head off! I'll go and show him what good shape I'm in, at seventy-seven." You looked so humiliated when I walked through the door, I almost wished I hadn't come. There was too much suffering in your eyes for me to enjoy the situation the way I thought I would. How long did I stay with you that day, maybe two hours? And you didn't manage to say ten sentences. I could read the humiliation on your face because you still had periods when you were completely conscious, totally aware, and I could see you were mortified to have me, who you always thought was so dumb, so thick, see you like that ... I wanted to take advantage of the occasion ... that's what I came for, but I couldn't! To see a human being in that state ... So young! So young! To see him concentrate for ten seconds so he could say hello, and then come out with "jello" instead ... I couldn't enjoy it. At one point, during a silence that lasted too long, I could see in your eyes that you thought I was happy to see you like that, that I was staying here so I could enjoy your humiliation, and that I wasn't leaving because I was happy you were aphasic. And you know what? I found that so outrageous, I didn't even bother to contradict you, or to defend myself. I thought, "If he's dumb enough to think that, let him think it. I'm not gonna try to tell him that, as usual, he only guessed part of what's going on, and he's happy to exaggerate the rest." But were you the one who was right, in the end? What do you think? Was I just ashamed to admit to myself something I found too ugly? Deep down inside, was I happy to see the challenger of the big, bad Dad reduced to mumbling a few garbled words in the hospital room where he was going to croak? Did I bury the pleasure I felt under the layer of pain, the layer of sadness a good father is supposed to feel under the circumstances? We'll never know, will we? Because it's too late for you, and because I'd never dare face something like that. Even if I find myself doing things since I started coming here, things I never would've imagined I could do. Talking like this, for instance, rattling on to a dying man who's lost his mind, talk, talk, talking till I drop, to an inert body, with no hope of settling anything, on your side or mine, because one of the partners has already checked out. I can finally tell you what I didn't dare tell you on television! Three times a week! I've come too late, I know, I'm sorry, really, I'm sorry, there's nothing I can do about it, and it pisses me off. I can feel myself getting soft when I see you, your limp body, your dirty diapers. I'd love to shout, "Tough luck for you, tough luck for you!" But I can't.

He takes a straight-backed chair and sets it down beside his son's wheelchair.

I got here one afternoon ... it smelled pretty bad ... it was actually goddamn awful ... I went to the nurse's desk to complain, I asked them again how they could leave my son like that when he needed to be cleaned up ... The nurse had bags under her eyes down to her knees, she told me she'd been working for eighteen hours straight, she could hardly stand up, she explained that there'd been emergencies, real emergencies, and your turn was coming, but not right away ... Well, I let her have it. I bet no nurse in the history of nursing has ever received as many insults as that nurse that day! I can't remember what I said to her, because you know how I can lose my temper when I'm really upset, but by the time I'd finished with her, she was ready to scrub the floor in your room every night after her shift! I finally told her to find me a wheelchair and a bathroom, on the double, because I wanted you to be clean within half an hour! I even asked her if I had the right to clean you up myself, and she said yes, but maybe I couldn't manage, because of my age, and the fact that you're no featherweight ... You know how I can't resist a challenge ... I came back here with a wheelchair, a little bar of soap and a towel ... Just transferring you from your bed to the wheelchair was quite a job, at one point I wondered what I'd gotten myself into, and thought maybe the nurse was right ... But I hate to admit someone else is right ... In the hallway, I looked like a good father, the nurse nodded at us and looked grateful when we went by. There was a doctor, too, who talked to me about your last play which he found a bit disappointing. And do you believe it, instead of being glad, I almost punched him in the nose! He even told me that everyone on the floor knew who you were ... I felt like saying, too bad that didn't get you any preferential treatment, that was clear from the way you smelled, but I bit my tongue, I just listened and gave him a dirty look ... I've always hated professional people and their condescending attitude, even when they're really nice! It's like they're stooping down to talk to you, for Chrissakes! Anyway, once we got to the bathroom, I realized that the person who'd taken a bath before you, or the nurse who'd given the bath, hadn't bothered to wash out the tub, so I had another fit. I went down the hallway shouting that I was going to file a complaint about the lack of cleanliness in the place, and believe you me, it wasn't long before two cleaning men showed up and got down on their hands and knees on the green tiles! No way I was going to bathe you in someone else's filth! I asked them to undress you and put you in the tub while they were at it, but they told me they weren't allowed to touch the patients ... So I did it myself! Undressing someone in a wheelchair isn't easy, even if they're only wearing pyjamas and a diaper ... It was the first time in my life I ever saw a dirty diaper, and it wasn't even a baby's diaper! I tried not to look at what I saw, to think of something else, but believe you me my nose brought me back to earth!

Seventy-seven years old, kid. Seventy-seven and I was able to undress you in your wheelchair, and to lift you up! I'm not saying it didn't take everything out of me, but I did it! And there I was in the middle of the bathroom holding my naked fifty-five-year-old son in my arms, I couldn't believe it, I never even gave you your bath when you were little! "To each his own job," I used to tell your mother, "and mine is to go out and earn the money to buy the diapers, it's your job to change them."

(*Silence.*) But I forgot to turn on the water first, how dumb can you get! So I had to set you down in the tub before I could turn on the faucet … (*Silence.*) I started to lather you, beginning with your head, your face, your neck … I left the water running, so you didn't smell so bad, and that was encouraging, even though my old back was killing me … (*Silence.*) After I lathered your chest, I noticed your legs … What a shock! You've got my legs, exactly the same legs as me! The same knees! The same feet! Even your pecker looks like mine. The two of us are identical from the waist down. You inherited your mother's face but your father's dick! And I sure hope you used yours as much as I

57

used mine! ... It was crazy! I felt like I was washing myself, but without feeling the soap on my thighs, my calves or my feet ... I've never liked the way hospital soap smells, but I'm telling you, that day I thought it smelled great! I closed your eyes so you wouldn't get soap in them ... I don't know if that's what you do with kids too ... Now I know every part of your body, like a mother with her baby. I know where you got your pigheadedness, but I wonder if you inherited more than a resemblance below the waist? Did you feel the same needs as me all your life? ... Guess we'll never know that either. Have you ever been forced to cover something up with Lotus, like I did? (*Silence.*) But ... (*Silence.*) It was there, bent over the bathtub, with the warm water running, rinsing, washing all the dirt away, that I felt myself soften up for the first time ... I don't know ... your skinny body, maybe, your bones sticking out everywhere, and you were so trusting, too, just like a sleeping baby ... I don't know ... (*Silence.*) I've always hated pity. I've always refused to pity people. You should never pity anybody! Ever! Otherwise, they'll devour you, and you'll end up disappearing, you'll forget yourself so you can take care of others, and other people don't deserve to be taken care of. Ever! (*Silence, then, very loudly.*) But you're my own kid! (*Silence.*) I said to myself, "Is today the day it's going to happen? Am I washing him so I can forgive him? Has the moment of forgiveness finally come?" If I wanted to, right then and there, bent over the bathtub, I had the strength to forgive you! I felt ... I don't know ... such a powerful feeling come over me suddenly ... I wished I could've done more than wash you ... I don't know ... hold you in my arms, kiss you ... But I didn't want to! I didn't want to soften up! I didn't want to feel pity! I thought, "Why should I forgive him? Why should I pity him when he's never pitied anyone in his life, he's always thought of himself, and fed off other people like a vulture? I shouldn't give in just because he's weak and defenceless. Even if he is my child. Even if he is my grownup fifty-five-year-old child." But I felt capable of doing it! I felt capable of forgiving you! And ... I don't know, I don't know what came over me ... I started to cry ... All of a sudden ... And I cried so hard! Over you! Over me! Over everything we never said to each other, during all those years, I guess … And maybe I was crying over my new weakness, too … I couldn't remember the last time I'd cried! I was brought up to think that men don't cry! And I still think that! But I couldn't stop! It was … uncontrollable! It came pouring out, like … like a river of tears! There I was, a man who'd always controlled everything in his life, facing something I really couldn't control. I was doubled over, I think I was even shouting! But I didn't want it to make me feel better. I refused to feel relieved! I didn't want relief! I didn't need relief, you did! Not me! Not me! I didn't want to see myself crying either, I didn't want to feel the tears running down my cheeks, it was too humiliating, so I turned on the shower … and tried to pretend the whole thing—my anger, my tears, my shouts—was just the water running down my face! It was the water from the shower that fell on your back, not my forgiveness! But I couldn't help it … I couldn't stop crying! I pressed my forehead against your chest … I was on the verge, I admit it, I was on the verge of begging for your forgiveness, and of forgiving you. Then suddenly, out of nowhere, without even looking for it, my hatred for you came back and hit me like a ton of bricks. Pity disappeared as fast as it had come, and I started to shake. Seconds before, I was crying out of pity, I was on the verge of forgiving you, and the next thing I knew, I was shaking with hatred! But where did all that come from? The pity? And the hatred? How can anyone hate his own kid that much? (*Silence.*) Is it because I knew that you'd been right all those years? That your plays … No. No. I refuse to think about that … (*Silence.*) I knew that if I wanted … It would've been so easy to kill you right then and there! Knock you out, on purpose, on the edge of the tub, or drown you … Then run to get help, crying, shouting there'd been an accident, and pass myself off as a hero, the good, seventy-seven-year-old father who wanted to wash his son but he was inexperienced, the poor man, and he drowned him. (*Silence.*) But … I refused to pity you, and killing you would've been like pitying you! So I stood up and went to get help. I was soaking wet, people could probably see I'd been crying, so I looked like a hero anyway, like a good father, a good Samaritan. (*Silence.*) When you're gone, it will be a relief, because you won't be able to hurt us anymore, to misrepresent us, or make up any more of your goddamn crazy stories ... I know you can't do anything now, you're a vegetable, you'll never get back to what you were before, I know you're not dangerous, but as long as you're still alive, I can still have reason to hate you ... But I'm tired. Once you're gone, maybe I'll manage to forgive you, but I'm not the one who's gonna help you leave out of pity! I can wait. If it doesn't take too long.

He stands up and walks away from his son.

But recently ... I don't know ... I can feel myself giving in. Seeing you in this state, or maybe because you're not aware of anything now, so you're no use to anyone ... I feel like I could do something irreparable ... And forgive you. Out of pity. Why? Because I'm fed up with coming here, or because I'm more human than I thought, or because I want to move on to something else. But what? You've been behind all the problems in my life for so long! Actually, the truth is ... it was easy to blame everything that went wrong in my life on you! And all my mistakes! When I'd find them in your plays, I could claim they were lies, and that was convenient, for sure! For thirty-five years now, you've been guilty of all my mistakes because you denounce them and then I can deny them, claiming you made them all up. What will I do when you're gone?

He comes back to his son, leans over his chair.

Go on! Leave! Stop hanging on! You're useless now that you're not aware of anything! I don't need you anymore. And I refuse, I refuse to pity you! Leave before I become human! If I forgive you while you're still alive, I'll never be able to forgive myself. Because it would be a weakness. The biggest weakness of all! Go on! Die! You're useless now. Die!

He straightens up, goes back to sit on the edge of his son's bed.

Sometimes, when I walk out of here, I'm convinced that you get out of your chair the minute I close the door, and that you start dancing, and laughing and clapping your hands. That you make fun of me like you did all your life. That you grab your notebook and start transcribing everything I just said. And I come racing back, I fling open the door … and I'm relieved every time!

He prepares to leave.

Enough of this emotional stuff, that'll do for today. Got to save some for next time … I didn't tell you about the weather … It's a strange day. The sky is completely white. Like there's a white bell over the city, and it hurts your eyes. The sun's not out, but you have to wear sunglasses … At least I do, it gives me migraines if I don't. (*Silence.*) I'll be back to give you your bath on Friday.

He exits.

CLAUDE remains alone for some fifteen seconds.

ALEX throws open the door and stares at his son.

Blackout. The End.